Wh
Muhammad

Peace Be Upon Him

Khurram Murad

The Islamic Foundation

Published by

THE ISLAMIC FOUNDATION,

Markfield Conference Centre,
Ratby Lane, Markfield, Leicester LE67 9SY, UK
Tel: (01530) 244944/5, Fax: (01530) 244946
E-mail:info@islamic-foundation.org.uk
Website: www.islamic-foundation.org.uk

Quran House, PO Box 30611, Nairobi, Kenya

PMB 3193, Kano, Nigeria

© The Islamic Foundation 1998/1419 H.
First published 1998, reprinted 2004/1425 H.; 2006/1427 H.

ISBN 0 86037 290 1

British Library Cataloguing in Publication Data
A Catalogue card for this book is available from the British Library

Typeset in Baskerville 11/14

Foreword

Khurram Murad has been a source of guidance and inspiration to thousands of people the world over. His death in December 1996 has deprived the *Ummah* of one of its great sons – a thinker, a prolific writer, a teacher, a guide and a leader of the Islamic movement. During the last months of his life he planned to write a trio on the Qur'an and the life and message of Prophet Muhammad *sallallaho ʿalaih wassallam*, particularly directed towards the Muslim youth in the English-speaking world. These small tracts were meant to reach the hearts and souls of our youth, yearning for guidance, seeking ideals to live by. *The Qur'anic Treasures* and *Gifts from Muhammad* were proof-read by him on his death bed. *Who is Muhammad* was still in the form of a first draft when he breathed his last. Now we are able to present this last work of Brother Khurram. We are grateful to Br. Abdur Rashid Siddiqui who has worked meticulously to edit and prepare this tract for publication. I have gone through the manuscript and made minor editorial modifications, keeping in view the purpose and style of Br. Khurram. I hope this small booklet will be of immense assistance to all those who want to understand Muhammad, *sallallaho ʿalaih wassallam*, the man and his mission.

Leicester   **Khurshid Ahmad**
11 April 1998

1

The Prophet Muhammad Today

One in every five persons on this earth firmly believes that the Prophet Muhammad is the last Messenger of God. He was a Muslim and there are more than 1.3 billion such Muslims today.

Not only individuals but entire countries take pride in declaring their allegiance to him. There are 54 such Muslim states today, ranging from those as large as Indonesia and Bangladesh, with populations of 200 and 125 million respectively, to those as tiny as the Maldives or Brunei with populations of 230,000 and 260,000. Even in non-Muslim countries, large Muslim populations constitute significant minorities; as much as 120 million in India and 20 million in China. Indeed, within the last half century, Islam, the religion brought by the Prophet Muhammad, has become the second largest religion in most European countries, as also in America and Canada.

Black and white, red and yellow, followers of the Prophet Muhammad come from all human races. Whether in Asia or Europe, Africa or America, in every nook and cranny of this globe, you are sure to find Muslims. They live in the most advanced, sprawling megalopolis as well as in the most primitive nomadic tent, village, hamlet, and even in the bush.

As now so always, down the centuries, across the planet, from end to end, billions and billions of men and women have lived all their lives, loving the Prophet and trying to follow in his footsteps, as no one else has been so loved and followed. They have lived and died, believed and acted, married and raised families, worshipped and ruled, made war and peace, even eaten and dressed, walked and slept, just as he did or taught them to do.

Indeed, never in history has a man influenced mankind, even beyond his death, so deeply and so pervasively as he has. He brings light and peace to countless hearts and lives. They love him more dearly than their own selves. In him they find their greatest source of inspiration and guidance. He is the ultimate norm and the perfect example for them. Faith in him is their mainstay, and he is their chief source of support and comfort in all personal vicissitudes and tribulations. To him they also look to lead them through social and political turmoil. He has always inspired them to greater and greater heights of spiritual and moral upliftment and civilizational achievements. And still does.

In short, they believe that through him, a human like themselves, God has spoken to them, and guided him to live amongst them, setting an example and a model for all times to come. Even today he motivates and induces whole populations to yearn and strive to shape their private lives, politics and policies according to his teachings.

Who, then, is this man Muhammad?

2

Early Life in Makkah

It was in the year 570, after Jesus, that Muhammad was born in Makkah, in what is now Saudi Arabia. Arabia, by all accounts, is the cradle of the human race. All the oldest human remains so far found come from the area of its location.

Hemmed in by red, black and brown volcanic hills about 80 kilometres to the east of the Red Sea, stands the city of Makkah. It was then a small merchant town on the ancient 'incense' route through which passed the great trade caravans between the south and north.

However, Makkah was, and remains, important for an altogether different reason. For here lies the Ka'bah, the 'first House' ever set up for mankind to worship their only God. More than 1,000 years before the Prophet Solomon built the temple in Jerusalem, his ancestor, the Prophet Abraham, aided by his elder son the Prophet Ishmael, raised its walls on very ancient foundations.

Close by the Ka'bah lies the well called Zam Zam. Its origin, too, goes back to the Prophet Abraham's time. It was this well which sprang up miraculously to save the life of the infant Ishmael. In the words of the Bible:

> And God heard the voice of the boy; and the angel of God called to Hagar out of heaven, and said to her: 'What ails you, Hagar? Fear not, for God has heard the voice of the boy where he is. Arise, lift up the boy, and hold him in your hand; for I will make him a great nation. And God opened her eyes, and she saw a well of water; and she went, and filled the bottle with water, and gave the boy a drink. And God was with the boy; and he grew and dwelt in the wilderness, and became an archer. (*Genesis* 21: 17–20)

Or, as the Psalmist sings:

> As they pass through the dry Valley of Baca,
> it becomes a place of springs;
> the early rain fills it with pools.
> (*Psalms* 84: 6)

Makkah never had, nor does it have now, any worldly inducement to offer for settlement. It is a barren, desolate place, where even grass does not grow! There were springs and wells of abundant water nearby in Taif, and a short distance away in Madinah. But it was the first House of God, architecturally an unremarkable cube, but spiritually and civilizationally the most remarkable fountain and spring of life – which made it supremely important, a place of attraction for people from all over the world. Forever, therefore, Makkah has been a great centre of pilgrimage.

By the time Muhammad was born, the Ka'bah's latest guardians, the tribe of Quraysh, had more than 300 idols installed in and around the Ka'bah to be worshipped as lords, gods and intercessors besides the One God. Muhammad was a direct descendant of the Prophet Abraham through the Prophet Ishmael. He belonged to the financially poor but politically strong and noble clan of Banū Hāshim from the tribe of Quraysh. As guardians of the Ka'bah, the House of God and the centre of pilgrimage for all Arabia, the Quraysh ranked higher in dignity and power than any other tribe. Hashim held the high office of levying taxes and providing the pilgrims with food and water.

Muhammad was born an orphan. His father, Abdullah, died before he was born. His mother, Aminah, too, passed away when he was only six years old. Doubly an orphan, his grandfather, Abd al-Muttalib, took him into his care. Only two years later, however, the orphaned boy was bereaved of his grandfather as well, leaving him in the care of his uncle, Abu Talib.

After his birth, the infant child was sent to the desert to be suckled and weaned and to spend part of his childhood among one of the Bedouin tribes, Banī Sa'd ibn Bakr, who live in the southeast of Makkah. This was the usual custom of all the great families in Makkah.

As Muhammad grew up, to earn his livelihood he pastured sheep and goats, as have done most prophets. His uncle and guardian, Abu Talib, also took him along with him on his travels with the trade caravans to greater Syria. He, thus, gained experience in trading. Because of his great honesty and diligence and the business acumen he showed in trading, he was soon being sought after to take charge of other people's merchandise, i.e. for those who could not travel themselves, and to trade on their behalf.

At the age of 25, Muhammad married a lady named Khadijah. A widow, Khadijah was 15 years older than Muhammad. She was a rich merchant of Makkah, and Muhammad had managed some of her trade affairs. It was she who proposed marriage. Khadijah remained Muhammad's wife and his closest friend and companion all her life till her death 25 years later. She bore him six children, of whom four daughters survived.

Until he was 40, Muhammad led a very uneventful life, showing no signs of the Prophet in the making that he was suddenly to be. What set him apart from his compatriots was his absolute truthfulness, trustworthiness and integrity, his sense of justice and compassion for the poor, oppressed and downtrodden, as well as his total refusal to worship any idol or do anything immoral. He was popularly acclaimed for these qualities. *Al-Amīn*, the Trustworthy, the Honest, *al-Ṣādiq*, the Truthful, were the titles on everybody's lips for Muhammad, which itself means the Praised One.

At a very young age, Muhammad enthusiastically joined a pact of chivalry for the establishment of justice and the protection of the weak and the oppressed made by certain chiefs of the Quraysh. He took part in the Oath when they all vowed 'that henceforth they would stand together as one man on the side of the oppressed against the oppressor until justice was done, whether the oppressed were a man of the Quraysh or one who had come from abroad.'

In later years, at Madinah, Muhammad used to say: 'I was present in the house of Abd Allah ibn Jud'an at so excellent a pact that I would not exchange my part in it for a herd of red camels, and if now, in Islam, I were summoned to a similar pact, I would gladly respond.'

A testimony to Muhammad's character was given by his wife Khadijah as she comforted him at the time when the first Revelation came to him. He said later: 'I fear for my life.' She replied: 'By no means! I swear by God that God will never lose you. You join ties of relationship, you speak the truth, you bear people's burdens, you earn for the poor, you entertain guests, and you help against the vicissitudes which affect people's rights.'

Muhammad's wisdom was also acknowledged by all. Once, while repairing the Ka'bah, various clans of the Quraysh disputed violently as to who should have the honour of placing the Black Stone in its place. As they were about to unsheathe their swords and go to war, they made the Prophet their arbitrator and he brought them peace. He placed the Black Stone on his cloak and asked all the clan chiefs to hold its edges and raise it, and then he placed the Black Stone in its appointed spot with his own hands.

3

The Prophet at Makkah

Muhammad was not only a wise, just, compassionate, honoured and respected man, but also a profoundly contemplative and spiritual person. As he approached the age of 40, increasingly he came to spend more and more of his time in retreat, in contemplation, worship, prayer, in the Cave of Hira in Jabal al-Nur, sometimes for several days at a time.

It was here that one night before dawn, in the last part of the month of Ramadan, the holy month of fasting for Muslims, the Angel Gabriel appeared before him in the form of a man, and said to him: 'Read', and the Prophet said: 'I am not a reader.' Thereupon, as he himself told it, 'the Angel Jibrail overwhelmed me in his embrace until I reached the limit of my endurance. Then he returned me and said: 'Read.' Again I said: 'I am not a reader.' Thrice the same thing happened. The third time, after releasing me from his embrace, the Angel finally said:

> Read in the name of your Lord Who has created. He has created man from a clot of blood. Read, and your Lord is the Most Bountiful: He who has taught by the pen, taught man what he knew not. (al-'Alaq 96: 1–5)

He recited these words after the Angel. And, then, the Angel said to him: 'You are the Messenger of God.'

Overawed by the unique experience of the Divine and overwhelmed by the huge burden of truth and message, he came out of the cave, his body trembling and his heart quaking. The Prophet returned home. 'Cover me! Cover me!', he said to his wife Khadijah. She quickly covered him with a cloak. Wrapped in the cloak, he told her what had happened in the Cave of Hira, how he had come to be appointed as God's Messenger.

The event in Hira, as narrated by Muhammad, was the supreme and most crucial event of his life. All that happened later has been happening over the centuries, and all the positions that he enjoys in the eyes of his followers, or his detractors, hinges on the veracity, truthfulness, authenticity and nature of this event in Hira.

Yet the only thing to support his claim in this respect was and remains his own word. Was he truly a Messenger of God? Was what he saw real and true? Or, was it an hallucination? Was he a man possessed? Did he just compose in words as poets do, the ideas he found in his heart?

These questions are raised today, as they were raised by his compatriots then. Of these his wife of 15 years was to be the first judge. She knew him too well to doubt even for a moment that he could say anything but the truth. She also knew his character. So, she believed in him without a moment's hesitation.

As with his wife Khadijah, so his closest friend

Abu Bakr, his adopted son Zayd, his cousin Ali who lived with him, in short all who knew the Prophet most intimately, believed in his truthfulness most spontaneously.

Khadijah took the Prophet to her cousin Waraqah, who had converted to Christianity, and acquired great learning in Christian Scriptures. Both the Jews and Christians had been expecting the coming of the last Prophet as foretold in their Scriptures. Had not Moses, just before he died, been told: 'I will raise up for them a prophet like you from among their brethren; and I will put my words in his mouth' (*Deuteronomy* 18: 18)? Who could be the brethren of the sons of Israel except the sons of Ishmael?

Who could be the mysterious Shiloh but the Prophet Muhammad, about whom Jacob prophesied immediately before his death, that to him would be transferred the Divine mission in 'the latter days': 'And Jacob called his sons and said, gather yourselves together, that I may tell you that which shall befall you in the last days . . . The sceptre shall not depart from Judah, nor a lawgiver from between his feet, until Shiloh come; and unto him the gathering of the people be.' (*Genesis* 49: 1, 10)

And, whom did Jesus mean other than Muhammad when he said: 'If I do not go away, the Helper will not come to you . . . he will not speak on his own authority, but whatever he hears he will speak' (*John* 16: 7–14)?

Waraqah therefore had no doubts that the last Prophet had come; so, he, too, believed in him.

But most of the people of Makkah who had acclaimed him as the Trustworthy (*Al-Amin*) and the Truthful (*Al-Sadiq*) could not bring themselves to believe in him. Nor could the Jews and Christians who had for so long been living in expectation of his arrival. Not that they doubted his truthfulness or integrity. But they were not prepared to turn their whole established way of life upside down by submitting to his simple but radical message:

When I recite the Qur'an, I find the following clear instructions: God is He who has created you, and the heavens and the earth, He is your only Lord and Master. Surrender your beings and your lives totally to Him alone, and worship and serve no one but Him. Let God be the only God.

The words I speak, He places in my mouth, I speak on His authority. Obey me and forsake all false claimants to human obedience. Everything in the heavens and on earth belongs to God; no man has a right to be master of another man, to spread oppression and corruption on earth. An eternal life beyond awaits you; where you will meet God face to face, and your life will be judged; for that you must prepare.

This simple message shook the very foundations of the Makkan society as well as the seventh-century world. That world, as today, lived under the yoke of many false gods: kings and emperors, priests and monks, feudal lords and rich businessmen, soothsayers and spell-binders who claimed to know what others knew not — all lorded over man. Not only that: man-made gods of their own desires, their tribal loyalties, their ancestors, and the powers of nature, like the nations, cultures, science and technology today all lorded over man.

The Prophet's message challenged them all, exposed them all, threatened them all. His immediate opponents in Makkah could do no better than brand him unconvincingly as a liar, a poet, a soothsayer, a man possessed. But how could he who was illiterate, he who had never composed a single verse, he who had shown no inclination to lead men, suddenly, have words flowing from his lips, so full of wisdom and light, morally so uplifting, specifically so enlivening, so beautiful and powerful, that they began to change the hearts and minds and lives of the hearers? His detractors and opponents had no answer. When challenged to produce anything even remotely similar to the words Muhammad claimed he was receiving from God, they could not match God's words.

First privately, then publicly, the Prophet continued to proclaim his Message. He himself had an intense, living relationship with God, totally committed to the Message and mission entrusted to him. Slowly and gradually, people came forward and embraced Islam. They came from all walks of life – chiefs and slaves, businessmen and artisans, men and women – most of them young.

Some simply heard the Qur'an, and that was enough to transform them. Some saw the Prophet, and were immediately captivated by the light of mercy, generosity and humanity that was visible in his manners and morals, in his words and works, and in his face too.

So also the opposition continued to harden and sharpen. It grew furious and ferocious. Those who joined the Prophet as also the Prophet himself were tortured in innumerable ways: they were mocked, abused, beaten, flogged, imprisoned, and boycotted. Some were subjected to much more inhuman tortures: made to lie on burning coal fires until the melting body fat extinguished them, or were dragged over burning sand and rocks. Yet such was the strength of their faith that none of them gave it up in the face of such trials and tribulations.

However, as the persecutions became unbearable, the Prophet said to them: 'If you go to Abyssinia, you will find there a king, a Christian, under whom no one suffers wrong.' About 80 of his followers, therefore, forsook their homes and emigrated to Abyssinia, where the Christian king gave them full protection despite the pleadings and machinations of the emissaries sent by the Quraysh chiefs. This was the first emigration of Islam.

All the while, the Prophet and his Companions continued to nourish their souls and intellects and strengthen their character and resolve for the great task that lay ahead. They met regularly, especially at a house near the Ka'bah called *Dar al-Arqam*, to read and study the Qur'an, to worship and pray, and to forge the ties of brotherhood.

Ten years passed, but the people of Makkah would not give their allegiance to the Prophet's Message nor showed any signs of mitigating their persecution. At the same time, the Prophet lost his closest Companions and his wife Khadijah, as also his uncle Abu Talib, his chief protector in the tribal world of Makkah.

The Prophet now decided to carry his Message to the people of the nearby town of Taif, known for its wealth. In Taif, too, the tribal leaders mocked and ridiculed him and rejected his Message. They also stirred up their slaves and the street urchins to insult him, mock him, and throw stones at him. Thus, he was stoned until he bled and was driven out of Taif. And yet when his Companion, Zayd, requested him to curse the people of Taif, and when God placed at his command the Angel of Mountains to crush the valley of Taif if he so wished, he only prayed for their being guided. Such was the mercy and compassion of the one who is the 'mercy for all the worlds'.

The Taif episode was the hardest moment in the Prophet's life. It signalled the advent of a new era for him, when his mission was to find a secure base, and was to ascend higher and higher in the coming days until the end of time.

To mark that, one night the Prophet was awakened and taken, in the company of the Angel Gabriel, first to Jerusalem. There he was met by all the Prophets, who gathered together behind him as he prayed on the rock in the centre of the site of the Temple, the spot where the Dome of the Rock stands today. From the rock, led by the Archangel, he ascended through the seven heavens and beyond.

Thus he saw whatever God made him see, the heavenly worlds which no human eye can see, and which were the focus of his Message and mission.

During this journey, the five daily Prayers were ordained for his people. Furthermore, it was then that the Prophet was given the charter for the new society and state soon to be born, which, too, was prophesied and which is described in *Surah al-Isra'* (Chapter 17) of the Qur'an.

4

The Prophet at Madinah

The Message that Makkah and Taif rejected, found responsive hearts in Yathrib, a small oasis about 400 kilometres to the north of Makkah. Now known as *Madinatun Nabi*, the city of the Prophet, or *Madinah Munawwara*, the radiant city, it was destined to be the centre of the Divine light that was to spread to all parts of the world for all times to come.

In quick succession, the Prophet suffered the terrible loss of Khadijah, his intimate and beloved companion for 25 years, and of Abu Talib, his guardian and protector against the bloodthirsty Makkan foes, and encountered the worst ever rejection, humiliation and persecution at nearby

Taif. As the Prophet reached the lowest point in his vocation, God brought him comfort and solace. On the one hand, spiritually, He took him during the Night of the Ascension to the highest of highs, realities and divinities, face to face with the Unseen. And on the other, materially, he opened the hearts of the people of Yathrib to the Message and mission of Muhammad.

Soon after Muhammad's return from Taif and the Night Journey, at the time of the Pilgrimage, six men from Yathrib embraced Islam. They delivered the Message of Islam to as many as they could, and at the time of the next Pilgrimage in the year 621 CE, 12 persons came. They pledged themselves to the Prophet, that they would make no god beside God, that they would neither steal nor commit fornication, nor slay their infants, nor utter slanders, nor disobey him in that which is right. The Prophet said: 'If you fulfil this pledge, then Paradise is yours.' This time the Prophet sent Mus'ab ibn 'Umayr with them to teach them the Qur'an and Islam and to spread the Message of Islam.

More and more people over the course of a year – tribal leaders, men and women – in Yathrib became Muslims. At the time of the next Pilgrimage, they decided to send a delegation to the Prophet, make a pledge to him, and invite him and all Muslims in Makkah to Yathrib as a sanctuary and as a base for spreading the Divine Message of Islam.

In all 73 men and two women came. They met the Prophet at 'Aqabah. They pledged to protect the Prophet as they would protect their own women and children, and to fight against all men, red and black, even if their nobles were killed and they suffered the loss of all their possessions. When asked what would be theirs if they fulfilled their pledge, the Prophet said: 'Paradise'. Thus, the beginning was made, the foundations of the Islamic society, state and civilization were set.

The road was now open for the persecuted and tortured followers of the Prophet to come to the House of Islam, that was to be Madinah. He, therefore, instructed them to emigrate, and gradually most of them found their way to Yathrib.

Their Makkan foes could not bear to see the Muslims living in peace. They knew the power of the Prophet's Message, they knew the strength of those dedicated believers who cared nothing for the age-old Arab customs and ties of kinship, and who if they had to would fight for their faith. The Makkans sensed the danger that the Muslims' presence in Madinah posed for their northern trade caravan routes. They saw no other way to stop all this but to kill the Prophet.

Hence they hatched a conspiracy: one strong and well-connected young man was to be nominated by each clan, and all of them were to pounce upon and kill the Prophet one morning as he came out of his house, so that his blood would be on all the clans' hands. Thus, the Prophet's clan would have to accept blood-money in place of revenge.

Informed of the plot by the Angel Gabriel, and instructed to leave Makkah for Madinah, the Prophet went to Abu Bakr's house to finalize the travel arrangements. Abu Bakr was overjoyed at having been chosen for the honour and blessing of being the Prophet's Companion on this blessed and momentous, sacred and epoch-making journey. He offered his she-camel to the Prophet, but the Prophet insisted on paying its price.

On the fateful night, as darkness fell, the youths selected by the Quraysh leaders to kill the Prophet surrounded his house. They decided to pounce on him when he came out of his house for the dawn Prayers.

Meanwhile, the Prophet handed over all the money left by the Makkans with him for safe keeping to Ali. Ali offered to lie in the Prophet's bed. The Prophet slipped out of his house, threw a little dust in their direction, and walked past his enemies, whose eyes were still on the house.

He met Abu Bakr at his house, and they both travelled to a nearby cave, the Jabal Thur. When the Quraysh realized that the Prophet had evaded them, they were furious. They looked for him everywhere and on all roads; they also offered a reward of 100 she-camels for anybody who would bring them the Prophet, dead or alive.

A tribal chief, Suraqa, sighted the Prophet and followed him, hoping to earn the reward. The

Prophet, with bloodthirsty foes in pursuit and an uncertain future ahead of him in Madinah, told Suraqa: 'A day will soon come when Kisra's golden hand bracelet will be in Suraqa's hands.' Thereafter, Suraqa retreated, and the Prophet proceeded towards Madinah.

This was *Hijrah*, the emigration – a small distance in space, a mighty leap in history, an event that was to become a threshold in the shaping of the Islamic *Ummah*. This is why the Muslims date their calendar from *Hijrah*, and not from Hira or from the birth of the Prophet.

In Qubah, 10 kilometres outside Madinah, the Prophet made his first sojourn. Here he built the first mosque. Here he also made his first public address: 'Spread peace among yourselves, give away food to the needy, pray while people sleep – and you enter Paradise, the house of peace.'

Three days later, the Prophet entered Madinah. Men, women, children, the entire populace came out on the streets and jubilantly welcomed him. Never was there a day of greater rejoicing and happiness. 'Come is the Prophet! Come is the Prophet!', sang the little children.

The first thing the Prophet did after arriving in Madinah was to weld the Emigrants (called *Muhajirs*) and the hosts, called the Helpers (or *Ansar*) into one brotherhood. Still today this brotherhood remains the hallmark of the Muslims. One person from the Emigrants was made the brother of one from amongst the Helpers. The Helpers offered to share equally all that they possessed with the Emigrants.

So the Muslims were forged into a close-knit community of faith and brotherhood, and the structure of their society and polity was being built. The first structure was also raised. This was the Mosque, or *Masjid*, the building consecrated to the worship of One God – called *Masjid al-Nabawi*, the Prophet's Mosque. Since then the *Masjid* has also remained the hallmark of the Muslims' collective and social life, the convenient space for the integration of the religious and political dimensions of Islam, a source of identification, a witness to Muslim existence.

At the same time, steps were taken and the required institutions built to integrate the entire social life around the centre and pivot of the worship of One God. For this purpose, five daily Prayers in congregation were established.

Ramadan, fasting every day from dawn to sunset for an entire month, was also prescribed. Similarly, to establish 'giving' as the way of life, *zakat*, a percentage of one's wealth to be given in the way of God, was made obligatory.

As long as there was no different instruction from God, the Muslims followed the practices observed by the Jews and Christians. Hence, they used to pray with their faces turned towards Jerusalem. But soon this direction to which the Muslims faced in Prayer was changed from Jerusalem to Makkah. This historic episode signalled the formation of a new Muslim community, charged with Divine trust and the mission of God's guidance, replacing the earlier Jews and Christians, and following the most ancient message of Abraham, turning towards the most ancient House of God, built by him.

5

Attacks by the Makkans

The Prophet, after arriving in Madinah, first formed an alliance with the Jews. Next, he approached all the nearby tribes and tried to persuade them to make an alliance or at least enter into a no-war pact. Many did. Thus the small group evicted from Makkah assumed strategic importance.

The Makkans who had earlier planned to kill the Prophet, were now determined to annihilate this nascent community of Islam. Having failed in all other ways they decided on a military solution.

A heavily armed Makkan force marched towards Madinah in the second year after *Hijrah*, on the pretext of protecting their trade caravan. The Prophet, despite his community's small number and lack of arms, decided to face their threat boldly. On the 17th of Ramadan, at Badr, the two forces met and fought a battle in which 313 Muslims defeated the 1,000-strong Makkan army.

Seventy of the Makkan chiefs who had been most active and vehement in persecuting the Muslims were killed; many others were taken prisoner, later to be released for ransom. For the first time, prisoners of war were treated humanely and kindly; they were fed and housed in the same way as their captors ate and lived.

In the third year after *Hijrah*, a 3,000-strong Makkan force again marched on Madinah, both to avenge the defeat at Badr and to make another attempt to defeat the Muslims; 700 of them were mailed and 200 mounted. The Muslims numbered only 700. The two sides met just outside Madinah near the Uhud Mountain. The initial Muslim victory was, however, reversed; the Muslim contingent posted to protect the rear, violated the Prophet's instructions and abandoned its position. The Quraysh attacked from behind, and victory was turned into defeat, resulting in the deaths of about 65 Muslims. The Makkans, however, failed to pursue their advantage and clinch victory.

The Makkans now planned to make a final assault on Madinah to settle the matter once and for all. All Bedouin tribes, Jews, and hypocrites within Madinah joined forces with them. In the fifth year after *Hijrah*, 24,000 of them advanced on Madinah. It was impossible to fight them on the open battlefield, or defend Madinah which was without walls. The Muslims therefore defended themselves by digging ditches all round Madinah. After laying siege to Madinah for 25 days, due to inner dissension, lack of supplies, cold weather and high winds, the Makkan army was forced to withdraw. This was the turning point in the history of confrontation with the Makkans. Madinah was never to be attacked again.

From the beginning, the Jews were given full rights of citizenship, yet they still committed acts of treason and treachery. Some had to be expelled; some were killed as a result of judgements given by an arbitrator appointed by them. However, subsequent generations of Jews were never held responsible for the misdeeds of the Jews of Madinah, as they were in Christendom for 2,000 years, for the crucifixion of Jesus. Instead, the Muslims always treated them justly and kindly.

The next year, the sixth after *Hijrah*, the Prophet and 1,400 Companions journeyed to Makkah to perform *umrah*, the lesser Pilgrimage, in accordance with several traditions of the time. They were unarmed. The Quraysh chiefs, against all established and accepted traditions, refused them admission. However, the Quraysh were now so low in morale and strength that they had to sign a peace treaty with the Prophet, the Hudaybiyah Treaty.

Though the terms appeared highly unfavourable, even humiliating, for the Muslims, they made tremendous gains by virtue of this Treaty. They, who were driven out of Makkah and attacked thrice, were now recognized as an equal force, to be treated respectfully, taken seriously. Peace provided an opportunity for the wavering and the neutral, even the hostile, to witness Islam at first hand, and many sensed the imminent victory of Islam. The result was that many Makkans and Arab tribes either embraced Islam or made peace with the Prophet.

As soon as the Hudaybiyah Treaty was signed, the Prophet sent letters to various neighbouring Arab and non-Arab rulers, including Chosroes of Iran and Heraclitus of the Byzantine Empire. He invited them to Islam, and assured them that he did not covet their kingdoms or riches. They could retain both, but only if they surrendered themselves to serve and worship the One God.

The Quraysh, however, soon broke the Treaty of Hudaybiyah. It was, thus, time to deal with their continuing hostility. The Prophet marched to Makkah, and captured the town. The fall of Makkah witnessed unparalleled acts of mercy, forgiveness and generosity. Not a single drop of blood was shed. Everybody who remained indoors was granted security of life and property. The Prophet forgave all who had been his bitterest foes all his life, who had persecuted him and planned to kill him, who had driven him out of Makkah, and who had marched thrice to Madinah to defeat the Muslims.

The neighbouring Byzantine Empire now prepared to attack and destroy the Muslim community in Madinah. However, when the Prophet marched to Tabuk on the northern border, his determination, courage and timely response made the enemy lose heart and withdraw.

6

Society Building

Throughout those years, when the Prophet was surrounded by hostile forces and ultimately triumphed over them, he continued to purify the souls and uplift the morals of his followers and lay the foundations of a just and compassionate family, society and state. His mission was now complete: he had created a new man, and changed the lives of multitudes of men and women by bringing them in total surrender to their Creator. He had created a new society: one based on justice. In his own life example, and in the Qur'an, mankind was given the light and way of a godly life.

It is remarkable that this entire epoch-making revolution which transformed not only Arabia but all of mankind for all time to come and which heralded the birth of the most brilliant civilization in the world cost no more than 750 lives, mostly opponents, in the various battles. Yet the Prophet is sometimes maligned as a man of violence by those who have exterminated thousands of people in pursuit of their civilizational ideals.

The Prophet performed his only *Hajj* in the tenth year after migration to Madinah. In the Plain of Arafat, he gave a sermon of unsurpassable beauty and lasting value: 'No man has any right to lord over other men; all men are equal, whatever their origin, colour or nationality.'

A few months later, in the eleventh year after *Hijrah*, the Prophet Muhammad died. He was buried in the house in which he had lived in Madinah.

The Prophet possessed a character of exquisite beauty and charm. He was merciful, kind and compassionate. He loved children and taught kindness to animals. He spoke softly, never abused anyone, forgave even his worst enemies. He lived a very simple life. He repaired his own shoes and clothes. He lived frugally, sometimes for days no food was cooked in his household.

Such is Muhammad. According to every standard by which human greatness can be measured he was matchless; no man was ever greater!